I am entrusting my life, love
and legacy journal to:

_____

HONORING

*Ms. Bee*

# Beloved,

My sincerest hope is that you will experience a calm release as you fill each page of this journal and give peace, love, and light to your family members who will read and savor every single word. So, fill each page one day at a time with your rich history, memories, and deepest desires for your legacy.

This journal is not meant to tell your entire life story as your family already knows it. However, it will inspire you to add your fondest thoughts, memories, and daily reflections, to help your family unlock even more about you and to carry them through their darkest hours after you have transitioned.

Fondly and with a full heart,

*Kinyatta*

# The Dash Poem
## (By Linda Ellis)

I read of a man who stood to speak
At the funeral of a friend
He referred to the dates on the tombstone
From the beginning...to the end

He noted that first came the date of birth
And spoke the following date with tears,
But he said what mattered most of all
Was the dash between those years

For that dash represents all the time
That they spent alive on earth.
And now only those who loved them
Know what that little line is worth

For it matters not, how much we own,
The cars...the house...the cash.
What matters is how we live and love
And how we spend our dash.

So, think about this long and hard.
Are there things you'd like to change?
For you never know how much time is left
That can still be rearranged.

If we could just slow down enough
To consider what's true and real
And always try to understand
The way other people feel.

And be less quick to anger
And show appreciation more
And love the people in our lives
Like we've never loved before.

If we treat each other with respect
And more often wear a smile,
Remembering this special dash
Might only last a little while

So, when your eulogy is being read
With your life's actions to rehash...
Would you be proud of the things they say
About how you spent YOUR dash?

Affix the image that you want to be remembered by here.

To my beloved Spouse/Life Partner/Significant Other:

**Always remember...**

To my beloved Spouse/Life Partner/Significant Other:

**Always remember...**

To my beloved Spouse/Life Partner/Significant Other:

**Always remember...**

_____
_____
_____
_____
_____
_____
_____
_____
_____
_____
_____
_____
_____
_____
_____
_____
_____
_____
_____
_____
_____

To my beloved Spouse/Life Partner/Significant Other:

**Always remember...**

To my beloved Son (s):

**Always remember...**

To my beloved Son (s):

**Always remember...**

To my beloved Son (s):

## Always remember...

_____
_____
_____
_____
_____
_____
_____
_____
_____
_____
_____
_____
_____
_____
_____
_____
_____
_____
_____
_____
_____

To my beloved Son (s):

## Always remember...

To my beloved Daughter (s):

**Always remember...**

_____
_____
_____
_____
_____
_____
_____
_____
_____
_____
_____
_____
_____
_____
_____
_____
_____
_____
_____
_____
_____
_____
_____

To my beloved Daughter (s):

**Always remember...**

To my beloved Daughter (s):

**Always remember...**

_____
_____
_____
_____
_____
_____
_____
_____
_____
_____
_____
_____
_____
_____
_____
_____
_____
_____
_____
_____
_____
_____
_____

To my beloved Daughter (s):

**Always remember...**

_____
_____
_____
_____
_____
_____
_____
_____
_____
_____
_____
_____
_____
_____
_____
_____
_____
_____
_____
_____
_____
_____

To my beloved Parent (s)/Caregivers:

**Always remember...**

To my beloved Parent (s)/Caregivers:

**Always remember...**

To my beloved Parent (s)/Caregivers:

**Always remember...**

To my beloved Parent (s)/Caregivers:

**Always remember...**

To my beloved Extended Family Members:

**Always remember...**

To my beloved Extended Family Members:

**Always remember...**

_____
_____
_____
_____
_____
_____
_____
_____
_____
_____
_____
_____
_____
_____
_____
_____
_____
_____
_____
_____

To my beloved Extended Family Members:

**Always remember...**

To my beloved Extended Family Members:

**Always remember...**

_____
_____
_____
_____
_____
_____
_____
_____
_____
_____
_____
_____
_____
_____
_____
_____
_____
_____
_____
_____
_____
_____
_____

My fondest memories growing up...

My fondest memories growing up...

My fondest memories growing up...

_____
_____
_____
_____
_____
_____
_____
_____
_____
_____
_____
_____
_____
_____
_____
_____
_____
_____
_____
_____
_____
_____

My fondest memories of love, relationships/marriage...

My fondest memories of love, relationships/marriage...

___

My fondest memories of love, relationships/marriage…

My fondest memories of my education and career...

_____
_____
_____
_____
_____
_____
_____
_____
_____
_____
_____
_____
_____
_____
_____
_____
_____
_____
_____
_____

My fondest memories of my education and career...

My fondest memories of my education and career...

_____
_____
_____
_____
_____
_____
_____
_____
_____
_____
_____
_____
_____
_____
_____
_____
_____
_____
_____
_____
_____
_____

Hobbies I enjoyed most...

Hobbies I enjoyed most...

___

Hobbies I enjoyed most...

Entertainment and entertainers I enjoyed most...

Entertainment and entertainers I enjoyed most...

Entertainment and entertainers I enjoyed most...

I want you to know this about spirituality and religion:

I want you to know this about spirituality and religion:

I want you to know this about spirituality and religion:

_____
_____
_____
_____
_____
_____
_____
_____
_____
_____
_____
_____
_____
_____
_____
_____
_____
_____
_____
_____
_____
_____
_____

My greatest fears...

My greatest fears...

_____
_____
_____
_____
_____
_____
_____
_____
_____
_____
_____
_____
_____
_____
_____
_____
_____
_____
_____
_____
_____

My greatest fears…

My greatest accomplishments…

My greatest accomplishments...

My greatest accomplishments...

I know that I will be loved and remembered most by...

___

I know that I will be loved and remembered most by...

I know that I will be loved and remembered most by...

_____

_____

_____

_____

_____

_____

_____

_____

_____

_____

_____

_____

_____

_____

_____

_____

_____

_____

_____

_____

_____

I always wanted to accomplish...

I always wanted to accomplish...

_____
_____
_____
_____
_____
_____
_____
_____
_____
_____
_____
_____
_____
_____
_____
_____
_____
_____
_____
_____
_____

I always wanted to accomplish...

My INCOMPLETE Bucket List includes…

_____
_____
_____
_____
_____
_____
_____
_____
_____
_____
_____
_____
_____
_____
_____
_____
_____
_____
_____
_____
_____
_____
_____

My INCOMPLETE Bucket List includes...

My favorite life quotes are...

I want to be remembered most for...

I want to be remembered most for...

_____
_____
_____
_____
_____
_____
_____
_____
_____
_____
_____
_____
_____
_____
_____
_____
_____
_____
_____
_____
_____

I want to be remembered most for...

My hope for my family after I have transitioned is…

My hope for my family after I have transitioned is…

My hope for my family after I have transitioned is…

_____
_____
_____
_____
_____
_____
_____
_____
_____
_____
_____
_____
_____
_____
_____
_____
_____
_____
_____
_____
_____

I lived my life according to these virtues...

I lived my life according to these virtues…

Honor my legacy by...

Honor my legacy by...

My beloved pet { insert name } loves to be…

_____
_____
_____
_____
_____
_____
_____
_____
_____
_____
_____
_____
_____
_____
_____
_____
_____
_____
_____

# While I'm Still Here...Self-Reflections

Date:      /      /

My plans for today included:
_____
_____

The most challenging part of today was:
_____
_____
_____

| **Today I feel:** |
| --- |
| ☐ At Peace |
| ☐ Fearful |
| ☐ Tired |
| ☐ Lonely |
| ☐ Reflective |
| ☐ Forgiveness |
| ☐ Anger |
| ☐ Determined |

I discovered that I enjoy: _____
_____
_____
_____

Today, I ate: _____
_____
_____

Today, I dressed up and felt: _____
_____
_____

I had a medical appointment today and: _____
_____
_____

I felt loved and supported by: _____
_____
_____
_____

This is what I will remember most about today: _____
_____

# While I'm Still Here...Self-Reflections

Date:  /  /

My plans for today included:
_____
_____

The most challenging part of today was:
_____
_____
_____

**Today I feel:**
- ☐ At Peace
- ☐ Fearful
- ☐ Tired
- ☐ Lonely
- ☐ Reflective
- ☐ Forgiveness
- ☐ Anger
- ☐ Determined

I discovered that I enjoy: _____
_____
_____
_____

Today, I ate: _____
_____
_____

Today, I dressed up and felt: _____
_____
_____

I had a medical appointment today and: _____
_____
_____

I felt loved and supported by: _____
_____
_____
_____

This is what I will remember most about today: _____
_____

# While I'm Still Here...Self-Reflections

Date:      /      /

My plans for today included:
_____
_____

The most challenging part of today was:
_____
_____
_____

**Today I feel:**
- ☐ At Peace
- ☐ Fearful
- ☐ Tired
- ☐ Lonely
- ☐ Reflective
- ☐ Forgiveness
- ☐ Anger
- ☐ Determined

I discovered that I enjoy: _____
_____
_____
_____

Today, I ate: _____
_____
_____

Today, I dressed up and felt: _____
_____
_____

I had a medical appointment today and: _____
_____
_____

I felt loved and supported by: _____
_____
_____
_____

This is what I will remember most about today: _____
_____

# While I'm Still Here...Self-Reflections

Date:      /      /

My plans for today included:
_____
_____

The most challenging part of today was:
_____
_____
_____

**Today I feel:**
☐ At Peace
☐ Fearful
☐ Tired
☐ Lonely
☐ Reflective
☐ Forgiveness
☐ Anger
☐ Determined

I discovered that I enjoy: _____
_____
_____
_____

Today, I ate: _____
_____
_____

Today, I dressed up and felt: _____
_____
_____

I had a medical appointment today and: _____
_____
_____

I felt loved and supported by: _____
_____
_____
_____

This is what I will remember most about today: _____
_____

# While I'm Still Here...Self-Reflections

Date:  /  /

My plans for today included:
_____
_____

The most challenging part of today was:
_____
_____
_____

**Today I feel:**
- ☐ At Peace
- ☐ Fearful
- ☐ Tired
- ☐ Lonely
- ☐ Reflective
- ☐ Forgiveness
- ☐ Anger
- ☐ Determined

I discovered that I enjoy: _____
_____
_____
_____

Today, I ate: _____
_____
_____

Today, I dressed up and felt: _____
_____
_____

I had a medical appointment today and: _____
_____
_____

I felt loved and supported by: _____
_____
_____
_____

This is what I will remember most about today: _____
_____

# While I'm Still Here...Self-Reflections

Date:     /     /

My plans for today included:
_____
_____

The most challenging part of today was:
_____
_____
_____

**Today I feel:**
- ☐ At Peace
- ☐ Fearful
- ☐ Tired
- ☐ Lonely
- ☐ Reflective
- ☐ Forgiveness
- ☐ Anger
- ☐ Determined

I discovered that I enjoy: _____
_____
_____
_____

Today, I ate: _____
_____
_____

Today, I dressed up and felt: _____
_____

I had a medical appointment today and: _____
_____
_____

I felt loved and supported by: _____
_____
_____
_____

This is what I will remember most about today: _____
_____

# While I'm Still Here...Self-Reflections

Date:     /     /

My plans for today included:
_____
_____

The most challenging part of today was:
_____
_____
_____

**Today I feel:**
- ☐ At Peace
- ☐ Fearful
- ☐ Tired
- ☐ Lonely
- ☐ Reflective
- ☐ Forgiveness
- ☐ Anger
- ☐ Determined

I discovered that I enjoy: _____
_____
_____
_____

Today, I ate: _____
_____
_____

Today, I dressed up and felt: _____
_____
_____

I had a medical appointment today and: _____
_____
_____

I felt loved and supported by: _____
_____
_____
_____

This is what I will remember most about today: _____
_____

# While I'm Still Here…Self-Reflections

Date:      /      /

My plans for today included:
_____
_____

The most challenging part of today was:
_____
_____
_____

**Today I feel:**
☐ At Peace
☐ Fearful
☐ Tired
☐ Lonely
☐ Reflective
☐ Forgiveness
☐ Anger
☐ Determined

I discovered that I enjoy: _____
_____
_____
_____

Today, I ate: _____
_____
_____

Today, I dressed up and felt: _____
_____
_____

I had a medical appointment today and: _____
_____
_____

I felt loved and supported by: _____
_____
_____
_____

This is what I will remember most about today: _____
_____

# While I'm Still Here...Self-Reflections

Date:     /     /

My plans for today included:
_____
_____

The most challenging part of today was:
_____
_____
_____

**Today I feel:**
- ☐ At Peace
- ☐ Fearful
- ☐ Tired
- ☐ Lonely
- ☐ Reflective
- ☐ Forgiveness
- ☐ Anger
- ☐ Determined

I discovered that I enjoy: _____
_____
_____
_____

Today, I ate: _____
_____
_____

Today, I dressed up and felt: _____
_____
_____

I had a medical appointment today and: _____
_____
_____

I felt loved and supported by: _____
_____
_____
_____

This is what I will remember most about today: _____
_____

# While I'm Still Here...Self-Reflections

Date:      /      /

My plans for today included:
_____
_____

The most challenging part of today was:
_____
_____
_____

**Today I feel:**
- ☐ At Peace
- ☐ Fearful
- ☐ Tired
- ☐ Lonely
- ☐ Reflective
- ☐ Forgiveness
- ☐ Anger
- ☐ Determined

I discovered that I enjoy: _____
_____
_____
_____

Today, I ate: _____
_____
_____

Today, I dressed up and felt: _____
_____
_____

I had a medical appointment today and: _____
_____
_____

I felt loved and supported by: _____
_____
_____
_____

This is what I will remember most about today: _____
_____

# While I'm Still Here...Self-Reflections

Date:     /     /

My plans for today included:
_____
_____

The most challenging part of today was:
_____
_____
_____

**Today I feel:**
☐ At Peace
☐ Fearful
☐ Tired
☐ Lonely
☐ Reflective
☐ Forgiveness
☐ Anger
☐ Determined

I discovered that I enjoy: _____
_____
_____
_____

Today, I ate: _____
_____
_____

Today, I dressed up and felt: _____
_____
_____

I had a medical appointment today and: _____
_____
_____

I felt loved and supported by: _____
_____
_____
_____

This is what I will remember most about today: _____
_____

# While I'm Still Here...Self-Reflections

Date:     /     /

My plans for today included: _____
_____

The most challenging part of today was: _____
_____
_____

**Today I feel:**
- ☐ At Peace
- ☐ Fearful
- ☐ Tired
- ☐ Lonely
- ☐ Reflective
- ☐ Forgiveness
- ☐ Anger
- ☐ Determined

I discovered that I enjoy: _____
_____
_____
_____

Today, I ate: _____
_____
_____

Today, I dressed up and felt: _____
_____
_____

I had a medical appointment today and: _____
_____
_____

I felt loved and supported by: _____
_____
_____
_____

This is what I will remember most about today: _____
_____

# While I'm Still Here...Self-Reflections

Date:       /       /

My plans for today included:
_____
_____

The most challenging part of today was:
_____
_____
_____

**Today I feel:**
☐ At Peace
☐ Fearful
☐ Tired
☐ Lonely
☐ Reflective
☐ Forgiveness
☐ Anger
☐ Determined

I discovered that I enjoy: _____
_____
_____
_____

Today, I ate: _____
_____
_____

Today, I dressed up and felt: _____
_____
_____

I had a medical appointment today and: _____
_____
_____

I felt loved and supported by: _____
_____
_____
_____

This is what I will remember most about today: _____
_____

# While I'm Still Here...Self-Reflections

Date:       /       /

My plans for today included:
_____
_____

The most challenging part of today was:
_____
_____
_____

**Today I feel:**
☐ At Peace
☐ Fearful
☐ Tired
☐ Lonely
☐ Reflective
☐ Forgiveness
☐ Anger
☐ Determined

I discovered that I enjoy: _____
_____
_____
_____

Today, I ate: _____
_____
_____

Today, I dressed up and felt: _____
_____

I had a medical appointment today and: _____
_____
_____

I felt loved and supported by: _____
_____
_____

This is what I will remember most about today: _____
_____

# While I'm Still Here...Self-Reflections

Date:      /      /

My plans for today included:
_____
_____

The most challenging part of today was:
_____
_____
_____

**Today I feel:**
- ☐ At Peace
- ☐ Fearful
- ☐ Tired
- ☐ Lonely
- ☐ Reflective
- ☐ Forgiveness
- ☐ Anger
- ☐ Determined

I discovered that I enjoy: _____
_____
_____
_____

Today, I ate: _____
_____
_____

Today, I dressed up and felt: _____
_____
_____

I had a medical appointment today and: _____
_____
_____

I felt loved and supported by: _____
_____
_____
_____

This is what I will remember most about today: _____
_____

# While I'm Still Here...Self-Reflections

Date:       /       /

My plans for today included:
_____
_____

The most challenging part of today was:
_____
_____
_____

**Today I feel:**
☐ At Peace
☐ Fearful
☐ Tired
☐ Lonely
☐ Reflective
☐ Forgiveness
☐ Anger
☐ Determined

I discovered that I enjoy: _____
_____
_____
_____

Today, I ate: _____
_____
_____

Today, I dressed up and felt: _____
_____
_____

I had a medical appointment today and: _____
_____
_____

I felt loved and supported by: _____
_____
_____
_____

This is what I will remember most about today: _____
_____

# While I'm Still Here...Self-Reflections

Date:      /      /

My plans for today included:
_____
_____

The most challenging part of today was:
_____
_____
_____

**Today I feel:**
☐ At Peace
☐ Fearful
☐ Tired
☐ Lonely
☐ Reflective
☐ Forgiveness
☐ Anger
☐ Determined

I discovered that I enjoy: _____
_____
_____
_____

Today, I ate: _____
_____
_____

Today, I dressed up and felt: _____
_____
_____

I had a medical appointment today and: _____
_____
_____

I felt loved and supported by: _____
_____
_____
_____

This is what I will remember most about today: _____
_____

# While I'm Still Here...Self-Reflections

Date: ___/___/___

My plans for today included:
_____
_____

The most challenging part of today was:
_____
_____
_____

**Today I feel:**
- ☐ At Peace
- ☐ Fearful
- ☐ Tired
- ☐ Lonely
- ☐ Reflective
- ☐ Forgiveness
- ☐ Anger
- ☐ Determined

I discovered that I enjoy: _____
_____
_____
_____

Today, I ate: _____
_____
_____

Today, I dressed up and felt: _____
_____

I had a medical appointment today and: _____
_____

I felt loved and supported by: _____
_____
_____

This is what I will remember most about today: _____
_____

# While I'm Still Here...Self-Reflections

Date:     /     /

My plans for today included:
_____
_____

The most challenging part of today was:
_____
_____
_____

**Today I feel:**
- ☐ At Peace
- ☐ Fearful
- ☐ Tired
- ☐ Lonely
- ☐ Reflective
- ☐ Forgiveness
- ☐ Anger
- ☐ Determined

I discovered that I enjoy: _____
_____
_____
_____

Today, I ate: _____
_____
_____

Today, I dressed up and felt: _____
_____
_____

I had a medical appointment today and: _____
_____
_____

I felt loved and supported by: _____
_____
_____
_____

This is what I will remember most about today: _____
_____

# While I'm Still Here...Self-Reflections

Date:      /      /

My plans for today included:
_____
_____

The most challenging part of today was:
_____
_____
_____

**Today I feel:**
☐ At Peace
☐ Fearful
☐ Tired
☐ Lonely
☐ Reflective
☐ Forgiveness
☐ Anger
☐ Determined

I discovered that I enjoy: _____
_____
_____
_____

Today, I ate: _____
_____
_____

Today, I dressed up and felt: _____
_____
_____

I had a medical appointment today and: _____
_____
_____

I felt loved and supported by: _____
_____
_____

This is what I will remember most about today: _____
_____

# While I'm Still Here...Self-Reflections

Date:      /      /

My plans for today included:
_____
_____

The most challenging part of today was:
_____
_____
_____

**Today I feel:**
- ☐ At Peace
- ☐ Fearful
- ☐ Tired
- ☐ Lonely
- ☐ Reflective
- ☐ Forgiveness
- ☐ Anger
- ☐ Determined

I discovered that I enjoy: _____
_____
_____
_____

Today, I ate: _____
_____
_____

Today, I dressed up and felt: _____
_____
_____

I had a medical appointment today and: _____
_____
_____

I felt loved and supported by: _____
_____
_____
_____

This is what I will remember most about today: _____
_____

# While I'm Still Here...Self-Reflections

Date:     /     /

My plans for today included:
_____
_____

The most challenging part of today was:
_____
_____
_____

**Today I feel:**
- ☐ At Peace
- ☐ Fearful
- ☐ Tired
- ☐ Lonely
- ☐ Reflective
- ☐ Forgiveness
- ☐ Anger
- ☐ Determined

I discovered that I enjoy: _____
_____
_____
_____

Today, I ate: _____
_____
_____

Today, I dressed up and felt: _____
_____
_____

I had a medical appointment today and: _____
_____
_____

I felt loved and supported by: _____
_____
_____
_____

This is what I will remember most about today: _____
_____

# While I'm Still Here…Self-Reflections

Date:      /      /

My plans for today included:
_____
_____

The most challenging part of today was:
_____
_____
_____

**Today I feel:**
☐ At Peace
☐ Fearful
☐ Tired
☐ Lonely
☐ Reflective
☐ Forgiveness
☐ Anger
☐ Determined

I discovered that I enjoy: _____
_____
_____
_____

Today, I ate: _____
_____
_____

Today, I dressed up and felt: _____
_____
_____

I had a medical appointment today and: _____
_____
_____

I felt loved and supported by: _____
_____
_____
_____

This is what I will remember most about today: _____
_____

# While I'm Still Here...Self-Reflections

Date:      /      /

My plans for today included:
_____
_____

The most challenging part of today was:
_____
_____
_____

**Today I feel:**
- ☐ At Peace
- ☐ Fearful
- ☐ Tired
- ☐ Lonely
- ☐ Reflective
- ☐ Forgiveness
- ☐ Anger
- ☐ Determined

I discovered that I enjoy: _____
_____
_____
_____

Today, I ate: _____
_____
_____

Today, I dressed up and felt: _____
_____

I had a medical appointment today and: _____
_____
_____

I felt loved and supported by: _____
_____
_____
_____

This is what I will remember most about today: _____
_____

# While I'm Still Here...Self-Reflections

Date:      /      /

My plans for today included:
_____
_____

The most challenging part of today was:
_____
_____
_____

**Today I feel:**
- ☐ At Peace
- ☐ Fearful
- ☐ Tired
- ☐ Lonely
- ☐ Reflective
- ☐ Forgiveness
- ☐ Anger
- ☐ Determined

I discovered that I enjoy: _____
_____
_____
_____

Today, I ate: _____
_____
_____

Today, I dressed up and felt: _____
_____
_____

I had a medical appointment today and: _____
_____
_____

I felt loved and supported by: _____
_____
_____
_____

This is what I will remember most about today: _____
_____

# While I'm Still Here...Self-Reflections

Date:      /      /

My plans for today included:
_____
_____

The most challenging part of today was:
_____
_____
_____

**Today I feel:**
- ☐ At Peace
- ☐ Fearful
- ☐ Tired
- ☐ Lonely
- ☐ Reflective
- ☐ Forgiveness
- ☐ Anger
- ☐ Determined

I discovered that I enjoy: _____
_____
_____
_____

Today, I ate: _____
_____
_____

Today, I dressed up and felt: _____
_____

I had a medical appointment today and: _____
_____

I felt loved and supported by: _____
_____
_____
_____

This is what I will remember most about today: _____
_____

# While I'm Still Here...Self-Reflections

Date:      /      /

My plans for today included:
_____
_____

The most challenging part of today was:
_____
_____
_____

**Today I feel:**
- ☐ At Peace
- ☐ Fearful
- ☐ Tired
- ☐ Lonely
- ☐ Reflective
- ☐ Forgiveness
- ☐ Anger
- ☐ Determined

I discovered that I enjoy: _____
_____
_____
_____

Today, I ate: _____
_____
_____

Today, I dressed up and felt: _____
_____
_____

I had a medical appointment today and: _____
_____
_____

I felt loved and supported by: _____
_____
_____
_____

This is what I will remember most about today: _____
_____

# While I'm Still Here...Self-Reflections

Date:      /      /

My plans for today included:
_____
_____

The most challenging part of today was:
_____
_____
_____

**Today I feel:**
- ☐ At Peace
- ☐ Fearful
- ☐ Tired
- ☐ Lonely
- ☐ Reflective
- ☐ Forgiveness
- ☐ Anger
- ☐ Determined

I discovered that I enjoy: _____
_____
_____
_____

Today, I ate: _____
_____
_____

Today, I dressed up and felt: _____
_____
_____

I had a medical appointment today and: _____
_____
_____

I felt loved and supported by: _____
_____
_____
_____

This is what I will remember most about today: _____
_____

# While I'm Still Here...Self-Reflections

Date:     /     /

My plans for today included:
_____
_____

The most challenging part of today was:
_____
_____
_____

**Today I feel:**
☐ At Peace
☐ Fearful
☐ Tired
☐ Lonely
☐ Reflective
☐ Forgiveness
☐ Anger
☐ Determined

I discovered that I enjoy: _____
_____
_____
_____

Today, I ate: _____
_____
_____

Today, I dressed up and felt: _____
_____
_____

I had a medical appointment today and: _____
_____
_____

I felt loved and supported by: _____
_____
_____

This is what I will remember most about today: _____
_____

# While I'm Still Here...Self-Reflections

Date:      /      /

My plans for today included:
_____
_____

The most challenging part of today was:
_____
_____
_____

**Today I feel:**
☐ At Peace
☐ Fearful
☐ Tired
☐ Lonely
☐ Reflective
☐ Forgiveness
☐ Anger
☐ Determined

I discovered that I enjoy: _____
_____
_____
_____

Today, I ate: _____
_____
_____

Today, I dressed up and felt: _____
_____
_____

I had a medical appointment today and: _____
_____
_____

I felt loved and supported by: _____
_____
_____
_____

This is what I will remember most about today: _____
_____

# While I'm Still Here...Self-Reflections

Date:    /    /

My plans for today included:
_____
_____

The most challenging part of today was:
_____
_____
_____

**Today I feel:**
- ☐ At Peace
- ☐ Fearful
- ☐ Tired
- ☐ Lonely
- ☐ Reflective
- ☐ Forgiveness
- ☐ Anger
- ☐ Determined

I discovered that I enjoy: _____
_____
_____
_____

Today, I ate: _____
_____
_____

Today, I dressed up and felt: _____
_____
_____

I had a medical appointment today and: _____
_____
_____

I felt loved and supported by: _____
_____
_____
_____

This is what I will remember most about today: _____
_____

# While I'm Still Here...Self-Reflections

Date:     /     /

My plans for today included: _____
_____
_____

The most challenging part of today was:
_____
_____
_____

**Today I feel:**
- ☐ At Peace
- ☐ Fearful
- ☐ Tired
- ☐ Lonely
- ☐ Reflective
- ☐ Forgiveness
- ☐ Anger
- ☐ Determined

I discovered that I enjoy: _____
_____
_____
_____

Today, I ate: _____
_____
_____

Today, I dressed up and felt: _____
_____
_____

I had a medical appointment today and: _____
_____
_____

I felt loved and supported by: _____
_____
_____
_____

This is what I will remember most about today: _____
_____

# While I'm Still Here...Self-Reflections

Date: ___ / ___ / ___

My plans for today included:
_____
_____

The most challenging part of today was:
_____
_____
_____

**Today I feel:**
- ☐ At Peace
- ☐ Fearful
- ☐ Tired
- ☐ Lonely
- ☐ Reflective
- ☐ Forgiveness
- ☐ Anger
- ☐ Determined

I discovered that I enjoy: _____
_____
_____
_____

Today, I ate: _____
_____
_____

Today, I dressed up and felt: _____
_____

I had a medical appointment today and: _____
_____

I felt loved and supported by: _____
_____
_____
_____

This is what I will remember most about today: _____
_____

# While I'm Still Here...Self-Reflections

Date:     /     /

My plans for today included:
_____
_____

The most challenging part of today was:
_____
_____
_____

**Today I feel:**
☐ At Peace
☐ Fearful
☐ Tired
☐ Lonely
☐ Reflective
☐ Forgiveness
☐ Anger
☐ Determined

I discovered that I enjoy: _____
_____
_____
_____

Today, I ate: _____
_____
_____

Today, I dressed up and felt: _____
_____
_____

I had a medical appointment today and: _____
_____
_____

I felt loved and supported by: _____
_____
_____

This is what I will remember most about today: _____
_____

# While I'm Still Here...Self-Reflections

Date:      /      /

My plans for today included:
_____
_____

The most challenging part of today was:
_____
_____
_____

**Today I feel:**
- ☐ At Peace
- ☐ Fearful
- ☐ Tired
- ☐ Lonely
- ☐ Reflective
- ☐ Forgiveness
- ☐ Anger
- ☐ Determined

I discovered that I enjoy: _____
_____
_____
_____

Today, I ate: _____
_____
_____

Today, I dressed up and felt: _____
_____
_____

I had a medical appointment today and: _____
_____
_____

I felt loved and supported by: _____
_____
_____
_____

This is what I will remember most about today: _____
_____

# While I'm Still Here…Self-Reflections

Date:      /      /

My plans for today included:
_____
_____

The most challenging part of today was:
_____
_____
_____

**Today I feel:**
☐ At Peace
☐ Fearful
☐ Tired
☐ Lonely
☐ Reflective
☐ Forgiveness
☐ Anger
☐ Determined

I discovered that I enjoy: _____
_____
_____
_____

Today, I ate: _____
_____
_____

Today, I dressed up and felt: _____
_____
_____

I had a medical appointment today and: _____
_____
_____

I felt loved and supported by: _____
_____
_____
_____

This is what I will remember most about today: _____
_____

# While I'm Still Here...Self-Reflections

Date:     /     /

My plans for today included:
_____
_____

The most challenging part of today was:
_____
_____
_____

**Today I feel:**
- ☐ At Peace
- ☐ Fearful
- ☐ Tired
- ☐ Lonely
- ☐ Reflective
- ☐ Forgiveness
- ☐ Anger
- ☐ Determined

I discovered that I enjoy: _____
_____
_____
_____

Today, I ate: _____
_____
_____

Today, I dressed up and felt: _____
_____
_____

I had a medical appointment today and: _____
_____
_____

I felt loved and supported by: _____
_____
_____
_____

This is what I will remember most about today: _____
_____

# While I'm Still Here…Self-Reflections

Date:       /       /

My plans for today included:
_____
_____

The most challenging part of today was:
_____
_____
_____

**Today I feel:**
- ☐ At Peace
- ☐ Fearful
- ☐ Tired
- ☐ Lonely
- ☐ Reflective
- ☐ Forgiveness
- ☐ Anger
- ☐ Determined

I discovered that I enjoy: _____
_____
_____
_____

Today, I ate: _____
_____
_____

Today, I dressed up and felt: _____
_____
_____

I had a medical appointment today and: _____
_____
_____

I felt loved and supported by: _____
_____
_____
_____

This is what I will remember most about today: _____
_____

# While I'm Still Here...Self-Reflections

Date:      /      /

My plans for today included:
_____
_____

The most challenging part of today was:
_____
_____
_____

**Today I feel:**
☐ At Peace
☐ Fearful
☐ Tired
☐ Lonely
☐ Reflective
☐ Forgiveness
☐ Anger
☐ Determined

I discovered that I enjoy: _____
_____
_____
_____

Today, I ate: _____
_____
_____

Today, I dressed up and felt: _____
_____
_____

I had a medical appointment today and: _____
_____
_____

I felt loved and supported by: _____
_____
_____

This is what I will remember most about today: _____
_____

# While I'm Still Here...Self-Reflections

Date:      /      /

My plans for today included:
_____
_____

The most challenging part of today was:
_____
_____
_____

**Today I feel:**
- ☐ At Peace
- ☐ Fearful
- ☐ Tired
- ☐ Lonely
- ☐ Reflective
- ☐ Forgiveness
- ☐ Anger
- ☐ Determined

I discovered that I enjoy: _____
_____
_____
_____

Today, I ate: _____
_____
_____

Today, I dressed up and felt: _____
_____
_____

I had a medical appointment today and: _____
_____
_____

I felt loved and supported by: _____
_____
_____
_____

This is what I will remember most about today: _____
_____

# While I'm Still Here...Self-Reflections

Date:       /       /

My plans for today included:
_____
_____

The most challenging part of today was:
_____
_____
_____

**Today I feel:**
- ☐ At Peace
- ☐ Fearful
- ☐ Tired
- ☐ Lonely
- ☐ Reflective
- ☐ Forgiveness
- ☐ Anger
- ☐ Determined

I discovered that I enjoy: _____
_____
_____
_____

Today, I ate: _____
_____
_____

Today, I dressed up and felt: _____
_____
_____

I had a medical appointment today and: _____
_____
_____

I felt loved and supported by: _____
_____
_____
_____

This is what I will remember most about today: _____
_____

# While I'm Still Here...Self-Reflections

Date:      /      /

My plans for today included:
_____
_____

The most challenging part of today was:
_____
_____
_____

**Today I feel:**
- ☐ At Peace
- ☐ Fearful
- ☐ Tired
- ☐ Lonely
- ☐ Reflective
- ☐ Forgiveness
- ☐ Anger
- ☐ Determined

I discovered that I enjoy: _____
_____
_____
_____

Today, I ate: _____
_____
_____

Today, I dressed up and felt: _____
_____
_____

I had a medical appointment today and: _____
_____
_____

I felt loved and supported by: _____
_____
_____
_____

This is what I will remember most about today: _____
_____

# While I'm Still Here...Self-Reflections

Date:      /      /

My plans for today included:
_____
_____

The most challenging part of today was:
_____
_____
_____

**Today I feel:**
☐ At Peace
☐ Fearful
☐ Tired
☐ Lonely
☐ Reflective
☐ Forgiveness
☐ Anger
☐ Determined

I discovered that I enjoy: _____
_____
_____
_____

Today, I ate: _____
_____
_____

Today, I dressed up and felt: _____
_____
_____

I had a medical appointment today and: _____
_____
_____

I felt loved and supported by: _____
_____
_____
_____

This is what I will remember most about today: _____
_____

# While I'm Still Here…Self-Reflections

Date:       /       /

My plans for today included:
_____
_____

The most challenging part of today was:
_____
_____
_____

**Today I feel:**
☐ At Peace
☐ Fearful
☐ Tired
☐ Lonely
☐ Reflective
☐ Forgiveness
☐ Anger
☐ Determined

I discovered that I enjoy: _____
_____
_____
_____

Today, I ate: _____
_____
_____

Today, I dressed up and felt: _____
_____
_____

I had a medical appointment today and: _____
_____
_____

I felt loved and supported by: _____
_____
_____
_____

This is what I will remember most about today: _____
_____

# While I'm Still Here...Self-Reflections

Date:      /      /

My plans for today included:
_____
_____

The most challenging part of today was:
_____
_____
_____

**Today I feel:**
- ☐ At Peace
- ☐ Fearful
- ☐ Tired
- ☐ Lonely
- ☐ Reflective
- ☐ Forgiveness
- ☐ Anger
- ☐ Determined

I discovered that I enjoy: _____
_____
_____
_____

Today, I ate: _____
_____
_____

Today, I dressed up and felt: _____
_____
_____

I had a medical appointment today and: _____
_____
_____

I felt loved and supported by: _____
_____
_____
_____

This is what I will remember most about today: _____
_____

# While I'm Still Here...Self-Reflections

Date:      /      /

My plans for today included:
_____
_____

The most challenging part of today was:
_____
_____
_____

**Today I feel:**
- ☐ At Peace
- ☐ Fearful
- ☐ Tired
- ☐ Lonely
- ☐ Reflective
- ☐ Forgiveness
- ☐ Anger
- ☐ Determined

I discovered that I enjoy: _____
_____
_____
_____

Today, I ate: _____
_____
_____

Today, I dressed up and felt: _____
_____
_____

I had a medical appointment today and: _____
_____
_____

I felt loved and supported by: _____
_____
_____
_____

This is what I will remember most about today: _____
_____

# While I'm Still Here...Self-Reflections

Date:      /      /

My plans for today included:
_____
_____

The most challenging part of today was:
_____
_____
_____

**Today I feel:**
- ☐ At Peace
- ☐ Fearful
- ☐ Tired
- ☐ Lonely
- ☐ Reflective
- ☐ Forgiveness
- ☐ Anger
- ☐ Determined

I discovered that I enjoy: _____
_____
_____
_____

Today, I ate: _____
_____
_____

Today, I dressed up and felt: _____
_____
_____

I had a medical appointment today and: _____
_____
_____

I felt loved and supported by: _____
_____
_____
_____

This is what I will remember most about today: _____
_____

# While I'm Still Here...Self-Reflections

Date:      /      /

My plans for today included:
_____
_____

The most challenging part of today was:
_____
_____
_____

**Today I feel:**
- ☐ At Peace
- ☐ Fearful
- ☐ Tired
- ☐ Lonely
- ☐ Reflective
- ☐ Forgiveness
- ☐ Anger
- ☐ Determined

I discovered that I enjoy: _____
_____
_____
_____

Today, I ate: _____
_____
_____

Today, I dressed up and felt: _____
_____
_____

I had a medical appointment today and: _____
_____
_____

I felt loved and supported by: _____
_____
_____
_____

This is what I will remember most about today: _____
_____

# While I'm Still Here...Self-Reflections

Date:      /      /

My plans for today included:
_____
_____

The most challenging part of today was:
_____
_____
_____

**Today I feel:**
- ☐ At Peace
- ☐ Fearful
- ☐ Tired
- ☐ Lonely
- ☐ Reflective
- ☐ Forgiveness
- ☐ Anger
- ☐ Determined

I discovered that I enjoy: _____
_____
_____
_____

Today, I ate: _____
_____
_____

Today, I dressed up and felt: _____
_____
_____

I had a medical appointment today and: _____
_____
_____

I felt loved and supported by: _____
_____
_____
_____

This is what I will remember most about today: _____
_____

# While I'm Still Here…Self-Reflections

Date:      /      /

My plans for today included:
_____
_____

The most challenging part of today was:
_____
_____
_____

**Today I feel:**
- ☐ At Peace
- ☐ Fearful
- ☐ Tired
- ☐ Lonely
- ☐ Reflective
- ☐ Forgiveness
- ☐ Anger
- ☐ Determined

I discovered that I enjoy: _____
_____
_____
_____

Today, I ate: _____
_____
_____

Today, I dressed up and felt: _____
_____
_____

I had a medical appointment today and: _____
_____
_____

I felt loved and supported by: _____
_____
_____
_____

This is what I will remember most about today: _____
_____

# While I'm Still Here...Self-Reflections

Date:    /    /

My plans for today included:
_____
_____

The most challenging part of today was:
_____
_____
_____

**Today I feel:**
- ☐ At Peace
- ☐ Fearful
- ☐ Tired
- ☐ Lonely
- ☐ Reflective
- ☐ Forgiveness
- ☐ Anger
- ☐ Determined

I discovered that I enjoy: _____
_____
_____
_____

Today, I ate: _____
_____
_____

Today, I dressed up and felt: _____
_____
_____

I had a medical appointment today and: _____
_____
_____

I felt loved and supported by: _____
_____
_____
_____

This is what I will remember most about today: _____
_____

# While I'm Still Here...Self-Reflections

Date:      /      /

My plans for today included:
_____
_____

The most challenging part of today was:
_____
_____
_____

**Today I feel:**
☐ At Peace
☐ Fearful
☐ Tired
☐ Lonely
☐ Reflective
☐ Forgiveness
☐ Anger
☐ Determined

I discovered that I enjoy: _____
_____
_____
_____

Today, I ate: _____
_____
_____

Today, I dressed up and felt: _____
_____
_____

I had a medical appointment today and: _____
_____
_____

I felt loved and supported by: _____
_____
_____
_____

This is what I will remember most about today: _____
_____

# While I'm Still Here…Self-Reflections

Date:      /      /

My plans for today included:
_____
_____

The most challenging part of today was:
_____
_____
_____

**Today I feel:**
☐ At Peace
☐ Fearful
☐ Tired
☐ Lonely
☐ Reflective
☐ Forgiveness
☐ Anger
☐ Determined

I discovered that I enjoy: _____
_____
_____
_____

Today, I ate: _____
_____
_____

Today, I dressed up and felt: _____
_____
_____

I had a medical appointment today and: _____
_____
_____

I felt loved and supported by: _____
_____
_____
_____

This is what I will remember most about today: _____
_____

# While I'm Still Here...Self-Reflections

Date: ____ / ____ / ____

My plans for today included:
_____
_____

The most challenging part of today was:
_____
_____
_____

**Today I feel:**
- ☐ At Peace
- ☐ Fearful
- ☐ Tired
- ☐ Lonely
- ☐ Reflective
- ☐ Forgiveness
- ☐ Anger
- ☐ Determined

I discovered that I enjoy: _____
_____
_____
_____

Today, I ate: _____
_____
_____

Today, I dressed up and felt: _____
_____
_____

I had a medical appointment today and: _____
_____
_____

I felt loved and supported by: _____
_____
_____
_____

This is what I will remember most about today: _____
_____

# While I'm Still Here...Self-Reflections

Date:      /      /

My plans for today included:
_____
_____

The most challenging part of today was:
_____
_____
_____

**Today I feel:**
☐ At Peace
☐ Fearful
☐ Tired
☐ Lonely
☐ Reflective
☐ Forgiveness
☐ Anger
☐ Determined

I discovered that I enjoy: _____
_____
_____
_____

Today, I ate: _____
_____
_____

Today, I dressed up and felt: _____
_____
_____

I had a medical appointment today and: _____
_____
_____

I felt loved and supported by: _____
_____
_____
_____

This is what I will remember most about today: _____
_____

# While I'm Still Here...Self-Reflections

Date:      /      /

My plans for today included:
_____
_____

The most challenging part of today was:
_____
_____
_____

**Today I feel:**
☐ At Peace
☐ Fearful
☐ Tired
☐ Lonely
☐ Reflective
☐ Forgiveness
☐ Anger
☐ Determined

I discovered that I enjoy: _____
_____
_____
_____

Today, I ate: _____
_____
_____

Today, I dressed up and felt: _____
_____
_____

I had a medical appointment today and: _____
_____
_____

I felt loved and supported by: _____
_____
_____
_____

This is what I will remember most about today: _____
_____

# While I'm Still Here...Self-Reflections

Date:       /       /

My plans for today included:
_____
_____

The most challenging part of today was:
_____
_____
_____

**Today I feel:**
☐ At Peace
☐ Fearful
☐ Tired
☐ Lonely
☐ Reflective
☐ Forgiveness
☐ Anger
☐ Determined

I discovered that I enjoy: _____
_____
_____
_____

Today, I ate: _____
_____
_____

Today, I dressed up and felt: _____
_____
_____

I had a medical appointment today and: _____
_____
_____

I felt loved and supported by: _____
_____
_____
_____

This is what I will remember most about today: _____
_____

# While I'm Still Here...Self-Reflections

Date:      /      /

My plans for today included:
_____
_____

The most challenging part of today was:
_____
_____
_____

**Today I feel:**
☐ At Peace
☐ Fearful
☐ Tired
☐ Lonely
☐ Reflective
☐ Forgiveness
☐ Anger
☐ Determined

I discovered that I enjoy: _____
_____
_____
_____

Today, I ate: _____
_____
_____

Today, I dressed up and felt: _____
_____
_____

I had a medical appointment today and: _____
_____
_____

I felt loved and supported by: _____
_____
_____

This is what I will remember most about today: _____
_____

# While I'm Still Here...Self-Reflections

Date:     /     /

My plans for today included:
_____
_____

The most challenging part of today was:
_____
_____
_____

**Today I feel:**
☐ At Peace
☐ Fearful
☐ Tired
☐ Lonely
☐ Reflective
☐ Forgiveness
☐ Anger
☐ Determined

I discovered that I enjoy: _____
_____
_____
_____

Today, I ate: _____
_____
_____

Today, I dressed up and felt: _____
_____
_____

I had a medical appointment today and: _____
_____
_____

I felt loved and supported by: _____
_____
_____
_____

This is what I will remember most about today: _____
_____

# While I'm Still Here...Self-Reflections

Date:      /      /

My plans for today included:
_____
_____

The most challenging part of today was:
_____
_____
_____

**Today I feel:**
- ☐ At Peace
- ☐ Fearful
- ☐ Tired
- ☐ Lonely
- ☐ Reflective
- ☐ Forgiveness
- ☐ Anger
- ☐ Determined

I discovered that I enjoy: _____
_____
_____
_____

Today, I ate: _____
_____
_____

Today, I dressed up and felt: _____
_____
_____

I had a medical appointment today and: _____
_____
_____

I felt loved and supported by: _____
_____
_____
_____

This is what I will remember most about today: _____
_____

# While I'm Still Here...Self-Reflections

Date: ___ / ___ / ___

My plans for today included:
_____
_____

The most challenging part of today was:
_____
_____
_____

**Today I feel:**
- ☐ At Peace
- ☐ Fearful
- ☐ Tired
- ☐ Lonely
- ☐ Reflective
- ☐ Forgiveness
- ☐ Anger
- ☐ Determined

I discovered that I enjoy: _____
_____
_____
_____

Today, I ate: _____
_____
_____

Today, I dressed up and felt: _____
_____
_____

I had a medical appointment today and: _____
_____
_____

I felt loved and supported by: _____
_____
_____
_____

This is what I will remember most about today: _____
_____

# While I'm Still Here...Self-Reflections

Date:     /     /

My plans for today included:
_____
_____

The most challenging part of today was:
_____
_____
_____

**Today I feel:**
☐ At Peace
☐ Fearful
☐ Tired
☐ Lonely
☐ Reflective
☐ Forgiveness
☐ Anger
☐ Determined

I discovered that I enjoy: _____
_____
_____
_____

Today, I ate: _____
_____
_____

Today, I dressed up and felt: _____
_____
_____

I had a medical appointment today and: _____
_____
_____

I felt loved and supported by: _____
_____
_____
_____

This is what I will remember most about today: _____
_____

# While I'm Still Here...Self-Reflections

Date:        /        /

My plans for today included:
_____
_____

The most challenging part of today was:
_____
_____
_____

**Today I feel:**
- ☐ At Peace
- ☐ Fearful
- ☐ Tired
- ☐ Lonely
- ☐ Reflective
- ☐ Forgiveness
- ☐ Anger
- ☐ Determined

I discovered that I enjoy: _____
_____
_____
_____

Today, I ate: _____
_____
_____

Today, I dressed up and felt: _____
_____
_____

I had a medical appointment today and: _____
_____
_____

I felt loved and supported by: _____
_____
_____
_____

This is what I will remember most about today: _____
_____

# While I'm Still Here...Self-Reflections

Date: ___ / ___ / ___

My plans for today included:
_____
_____

The most challenging part of today was:
_____
_____
_____

**Today I feel:**
- ☐ At Peace
- ☐ Fearful
- ☐ Tired
- ☐ Lonely
- ☐ Reflective
- ☐ Forgiveness
- ☐ Anger
- ☐ Determined

I discovered that I enjoy: _____
_____
_____
_____

Today, I ate: _____
_____
_____

Today, I dressed up and felt: _____
_____
_____

I had a medical appointment today and: _____
_____
_____

I felt loved and supported by: _____
_____
_____
_____

This is what I will remember most about today: _____
_____

# While I'm Still Here...Self-Reflections

Date:     /     /

My plans for today included:
_____
_____

The most challenging part of today was:
_____
_____
_____

**Today I feel:**
☐ At Peace
☐ Fearful
☐ Tired
☐ Lonely
☐ Reflective
☐ Forgiveness
☐ Anger
☐ Determined

I discovered that I enjoy: _____
_____
_____
_____

Today, I ate: _____
_____
_____

Today, I dressed up and felt: _____
_____
_____

I had a medical appointment today and: _____
_____
_____

I felt loved and supported by: _____
_____
_____
_____

This is what I will remember most about today: _____
_____

# While I'm Still Here...Self-Reflections

Date:      /      /

My plans for today included:
_____
_____

The most challenging part of today was:
_____
_____
_____

**Today I feel:**
- ☐ At Peace
- ☐ Fearful
- ☐ Tired
- ☐ Lonely
- ☐ Reflective
- ☐ Forgiveness
- ☐ Anger
- ☐ Determined

I discovered that I enjoy: _____
_____
_____
_____

Today, I ate: _____
_____
_____

Today, I dressed up and felt: _____
_____
_____

I had a medical appointment today and: _____
_____
_____

I felt loved and supported by: _____
_____
_____
_____

This is what I will remember most about today: _____
_____

# While I'm Still Here...Self-Reflections

Date:     /     /

My plans for today included:
_____
_____

The most challenging part of today was:
_____
_____
_____

**Today I feel:**
- ☐ At Peace
- ☐ Fearful
- ☐ Tired
- ☐ Lonely
- ☐ Reflective
- ☐ Forgiveness
- ☐ Anger
- ☐ Determined

I discovered that I enjoy: _____
_____
_____
_____

Today, I ate: _____
_____
_____

Today, I dressed up and felt: _____
_____
_____

I had a medical appointment today and: _____
_____
_____

I felt loved and supported by: _____
_____
_____
_____

This is what I will remember most about today: _____
_____

# While I'm Still Here...Self-Reflections

Date:      /      /

My plans for today included:
_____
_____

The most challenging part of today was:
_____
_____
_____

**Today I feel:**
☐ At Peace
☐ Fearful
☐ Tired
☐ Lonely
☐ Reflective
☐ Forgiveness
☐ Anger
☐ Determined

I discovered that I enjoy: _____
_____
_____
_____

Today, I ate: _____
_____
_____

Today, I dressed up and felt: _____
_____
_____

I had a medical appointment today and: _____
_____
_____

I felt loved and supported by: _____
_____
_____

This is what I will remember most about today: _____
_____

# While I'm Still Here...Self-Reflections

Date:      /      /

My plans for today included:
_____
_____

The most challenging part of today was:
_____
_____
_____

**Today I feel:**
- ☐ At Peace
- ☐ Fearful
- ☐ Tired
- ☐ Lonely
- ☐ Reflective
- ☐ Forgiveness
- ☐ Anger
- ☐ Determined

I discovered that I enjoy: _____
_____
_____
_____

Today, I ate: _____
_____
_____

Today, I dressed up and felt: _____
_____
_____

I had a medical appointment today and: _____
_____
_____

I felt loved and supported by: _____
_____
_____
_____

This is what I will remember most about today: _____
_____

# While I'm Still Here...Self-Reflections

Date:     /     /

My plans for today included:
_____
_____

The most challenging part of today was:
_____
_____
_____

**Today I feel:**
☐ At Peace
☐ Fearful
☐ Tired
☐ Lonely
☐ Reflective
☐ Forgiveness
☐ Anger
☐ Determined

I discovered that I enjoy: _____
_____
_____

Today, I ate: _____
_____

Today, I dressed up and felt: _____
_____

I had a medical appointment today and: _____
_____

I felt loved and supported by: _____
_____
_____

This is what I will remember most about today: _____
_____

# While I'm Still Here...Self-Reflections

Date:      /      /

My plans for today included:
_____
_____

The most challenging part of today was:
_____
_____
_____

**Today I feel:**
- ☐ At Peace
- ☐ Fearful
- ☐ Tired
- ☐ Lonely
- ☐ Reflective
- ☐ Forgiveness
- ☐ Anger
- ☐ Determined

I discovered that I enjoy: _____
_____
_____
_____

Today, I ate: _____
_____
_____

Today, I dressed up and felt: _____
_____
_____

I had a medical appointment today and: _____
_____
_____

I felt loved and supported by: _____
_____
_____
_____

This is what I will remember most about today: _____
_____

# While I'm Still Here...Self-Reflections

Date:      /      /

My plans for today included:
_____
_____

The most challenging part of today was:
_____
_____
_____

**Today I feel:**
☐ At Peace
☐ Fearful
☐ Tired
☐ Lonely
☐ Reflective
☐ Forgiveness
☐ Anger
☐ Determined

I discovered that I enjoy: _____
_____
_____
_____

Today, I ate: _____
_____
_____

Today, I dressed up and felt: _____
_____

I had a medical appointment today and: _____
_____

I felt loved and supported by: _____
_____
_____

This is what I will remember most about today: _____
_____

# While I'm Still Here...Self-Reflections

Date:      /      /

My plans for today included:
_____
_____

The most challenging part of today was:
_____
_____
_____

**Today I feel:**
- ☐ At Peace
- ☐ Fearful
- ☐ Tired
- ☐ Lonely
- ☐ Reflective
- ☐ Forgiveness
- ☐ Anger
- ☐ Determined

I discovered that I enjoy: _____
_____
_____
_____

Today, I ate: _____
_____
_____

Today, I dressed up and felt: _____
_____
_____

I had a medical appointment today and: _____
_____
_____

I felt loved and supported by: _____
_____
_____
_____

This is what I will remember most about today: _____
_____

# While I'm Still Here...Self-Reflections

Date:       /       /

My plans for today included:
_____
_____

The most challenging part of today was:
_____
_____
_____

**Today I feel:**
☐ At Peace
☐ Fearful
☐ Tired
☐ Lonely
☐ Reflective
☐ Forgiveness
☐ Anger
☐ Determined

I discovered that I enjoy: _____
_____
_____
_____

Today, I ate: _____
_____
_____

Today, I dressed up and felt: _____
_____
_____

I had a medical appointment today and: _____
_____
_____

I felt loved and supported by: _____
_____
_____
_____

This is what I will remember most about today: _____
_____

# While I'm Still Here...Self-Reflections

Date:      /      /

My plans for today included:
_____
_____

The most challenging part of today was:
_____
_____
_____

**Today I feel:**
- ☐ At Peace
- ☐ Fearful
- ☐ Tired
- ☐ Lonely
- ☐ Reflective
- ☐ Forgiveness
- ☐ Anger
- ☐ Determined

I discovered that I enjoy: _____
_____
_____
_____

Today, I ate: _____
_____
_____

Today, I dressed up and felt: _____
_____
_____

I had a medical appointment today and: _____
_____
_____

I felt loved and supported by: _____
_____
_____
_____

This is what I will remember most about today: _____
_____

# While I'm Still Here...Self-Reflections

Date:      /      /

My plans for today included:
_____
_____

The most challenging part of today was:
_____
_____
_____

**Today I feel:**
☐ At Peace
☐ Fearful
☐ Tired
☐ Lonely
☐ Reflective
☐ Forgiveness
☐ Anger
☐ Determined

I discovered that I enjoy: _____
_____
_____
_____

Today, I ate: _____
_____
_____

Today, I dressed up and felt: _____
_____
_____

I had a medical appointment today and: _____
_____
_____

I felt loved and supported by: _____
_____
_____

This is what I will remember most about today: _____
_____

# While I'm Still Here...Self-Reflections

Date:      /      /

My plans for today included:
_____
_____

The most challenging part of today was:
_____
_____
_____

**Today I feel:**
☐ At Peace
☐ Fearful
☐ Tired
☐ Lonely
☐ Reflective
☐ Forgiveness
☐ Anger
☐ Determined

I discovered that I enjoy: _____
_____
_____
_____

Today, I ate: _____
_____
_____

Today, I dressed up and felt: _____
_____
_____

I had a medical appointment today and: _____
_____
_____

I felt loved and supported by: _____
_____
_____
_____

This is what I will remember most about today: _____
_____

# While I'm Still Here...Self-Reflections

Date:      /      /

My plans for today included:
_____
_____

The most challenging part of today was:
_____
_____
_____

**Today I feel:**
☐ At Peace
☐ Fearful
☐ Tired
☐ Lonely
☐ Reflective
☐ Forgiveness
☐ Anger
☐ Determined

I discovered that I enjoy: _____
_____
_____
_____

Today, I ate: _____
_____
_____

Today, I dressed up and felt: _____
_____
_____

I had a medical appointment today and: _____
_____
_____

I felt loved and supported by: _____
_____
_____
_____

This is what I will remember most about today: _____
_____

# While I'm Still Here...Self-Reflections

Date:       /       /

My plans for today included:
_____
_____

The most challenging part of today was:
_____
_____
_____

**Today I feel:**
- ☐ At Peace
- ☐ Fearful
- ☐ Tired
- ☐ Lonely
- ☐ Reflective
- ☐ Forgiveness
- ☐ Anger
- ☐ Determined

I discovered that I enjoy: _____
_____
_____
_____

Today, I ate: _____
_____
_____

Today, I dressed up and felt: _____
_____
_____

I had a medical appointment today and: _____
_____
_____

I felt loved and supported by: _____
_____
_____
_____

This is what I will remember most about today: _____
_____

# While I'm Still Here…Self-Reflections

Date:        /        /

My plans for today included:
_____
_____

The most challenging part of today was:
_____
_____
_____

| Today I feel: |
| --- |
| ☐ At Peace |
| ☐ Fearful |
| ☐ Tired |
| ☐ Lonely |
| ☐ Reflective |
| ☐ Forgiveness |
| ☐ Anger |
| ☐ Determined |

I discovered that I enjoy: _____
_____
_____
_____

Today, I ate: _____
_____
_____

Today, I dressed up and felt: _____
_____
_____

I had a medical appointment today and: _____
_____
_____

I felt loved and supported by: _____
_____
_____
_____

This is what I will remember most about today: _____
_____

# While I'm Still Here...Self-Reflections

Date:      /      /

My plans for today included:
_____
_____

The most challenging part of today was:
_____
_____
_____

**Today I feel:**
- ☐ At Peace
- ☐ Fearful
- ☐ Tired
- ☐ Lonely
- ☐ Reflective
- ☐ Forgiveness
- ☐ Anger
- ☐ Determined

I discovered that I enjoy: _____
_____
_____
_____

Today, I ate: _____
_____
_____

Today, I dressed up and felt: _____
_____
_____

I had a medical appointment today and: _____
_____
_____

I felt loved and supported by: _____
_____
_____
_____

This is what I will remember most about today: _____
_____

# While I'm Still Here...Self-Reflections

Date:      /      /

My plans for today included:
_____
_____

The most challenging part of today was:
_____
_____
_____

**Today I feel:**
☐ At Peace
☐ Fearful
☐ Tired
☐ Lonely
☐ Reflective
☐ Forgiveness
☐ Anger
☐ Determined

I discovered that I enjoy: _____
_____
_____
_____

Today, I ate: _____
_____
_____

Today, I dressed up and felt: _____
_____
_____

I had a medical appointment today and: _____
_____
_____

I felt loved and supported by: _____
_____
_____
_____

This is what I will remember most about today: _____
_____

# While I'm Still Here…Self-Reflections

Date:      /      /

My plans for today included:
_____
_____

The most challenging part of today was:
_____
_____
_____

**Today I feel:**
☐ At Peace
☐ Fearful
☐ Tired
☐ Lonely
☐ Reflective
☐ Forgiveness
☐ Anger
☐ Determined

I discovered that I enjoy: _____
_____
_____
_____

Today, I ate: _____
_____
_____

Today, I dressed up and felt: _____
_____
_____

I had a medical appointment today and: _____
_____
_____

I felt loved and supported by: _____
_____
_____
_____

This is what I will remember most about today: _____
_____

# While I'm Still Here...Self-Reflections

Date:     /     /

My plans for today included:
_____
_____

The most challenging part of today was:
_____
_____
_____

**Today I feel:**
- ☐ At Peace
- ☐ Fearful
- ☐ Tired
- ☐ Lonely
- ☐ Reflective
- ☐ Forgiveness
- ☐ Anger
- ☐ Determined

I discovered that I enjoy: _____
_____
_____
_____

Today, I ate: _____
_____
_____

Today, I dressed up and felt: _____
_____
_____

I had a medical appointment today and: _____
_____
_____

I felt loved and supported by: _____
_____
_____

This is what I will remember most about today: _____
_____

# While I'm Still Here...Self-Reflections

Date:        /        /

My plans for today included:
_____
_____

The most challenging part of today was:
_____
_____
_____

**Today I feel:**
- ☐ At Peace
- ☐ Fearful
- ☐ Tired
- ☐ Lonely
- ☐ Reflective
- ☐ Forgiveness
- ☐ Anger
- ☐ Determined

I discovered that I enjoy: _____
_____
_____
_____

Today, I ate: _____
_____
_____

Today, I dressed up and felt: _____
_____
_____

I had a medical appointment today and: _____
_____
_____

I felt loved and supported by: _____
_____
_____
_____

This is what I will remember most about today: _____
_____

# While I'm Still Here...Self-Reflections

Date:      /      /

My plans for today included:
_____
_____

The most challenging part of today was:
_____
_____
_____

**Today I feel:**
- ☐ At Peace
- ☐ Fearful
- ☐ Tired
- ☐ Lonely
- ☐ Reflective
- ☐ Forgiveness
- ☐ Anger
- ☐ Determined

I discovered that I enjoy: _____
_____
_____
_____

Today, I ate: _____
_____
_____

Today, I dressed up and felt: _____
_____
_____

I had a medical appointment today and: _____
_____
_____

I felt loved and supported by: _____
_____
_____
_____

This is what I will remember most about today: _____
_____

# While I'm Still Here...Self-Reflections

Date:      /      /

My plans for today included:
_____
_____

The most challenging part of today was:
_____
_____

**Today I feel:**
- ☐ At Peace
- ☐ Fearful
- ☐ Tired
- ☐ Lonely
- ☐ Reflective
- ☐ Forgiveness
- ☐ Anger
- ☐ Determined

I discovered that I enjoy: _____
_____
_____
_____

Today, I ate: _____
_____
_____

Today, I dressed up and felt: _____
_____
_____

I had a medical appointment today and: _____
_____
_____

I felt loved and supported by: _____
_____
_____

This is what I will remember most about today: _____
_____

# While I'm Still Here...Self-Reflections

Date:     /     /

My plans for today included:
_____
_____

The most challenging part of today was:
_____
_____
_____

| Today I feel: |
|---|
| ☐ At Peace |
| ☐ Fearful |
| ☐ Tired |
| ☐ Lonely |
| ☐ Reflective |
| ☐ Forgiveness |
| ☐ Anger |
| ☐ Determined |

I discovered that I enjoy: _____
_____
_____
_____

Today, I ate: _____
_____
_____

Today, I dressed up and felt: _____
_____

I had a medical appointment today and: _____
_____

I felt loved and supported by: _____
_____
_____

This is what I will remember most about today: _____
_____

# While I'm Still Here...Self-Reflections

Date:     /     /

My plans for today included:
_____
_____

The most challenging part of today was:
_____
_____
_____

**Today I feel:**
☐ At Peace
☐ Fearful
☐ Tired
☐ Lonely
☐ Reflective
☐ Forgiveness
☐ Anger
☐ Determined

I discovered that I enjoy: _____
_____
_____
_____

Today, I ate: _____
_____
_____

Today, I dressed up and felt: _____
_____
_____

I had a medical appointment today and: _____
_____
_____

I felt loved and supported by: _____
_____
_____
_____

This is what I will remember most about today: _____
_____

# While I'm Still Here...Self-Reflections

Date:      /      /

My plans for today included:
_____
_____

The most challenging part of today was:
_____
_____
_____

**Today I feel:**
☐ At Peace
☐ Fearful
☐ Tired
☐ Lonely
☐ Reflective
☐ Forgiveness
☐ Anger
☐ Determined

I discovered that I enjoy: _____
_____
_____
_____

Today, I ate: _____
_____
_____

Today, I dressed up and felt: _____
_____
_____

I had a medical appointment today and: _____
_____
_____

I felt loved and supported by: _____
_____
_____
_____

This is what I will remember most about today: _____
_____

# While I'm Still Here...Self-Reflections

Date:        /        /

My plans for today included:
_____
_____

The most challenging part of today was:
_____
_____
_____

**Today I feel:**
- ☐ At Peace
- ☐ Fearful
- ☐ Tired
- ☐ Lonely
- ☐ Reflective
- ☐ Forgiveness
- ☐ Anger
- ☐ Determined

I discovered that I enjoy: _____
_____
_____
_____

Today, I ate: _____
_____
_____

Today, I dressed up and felt: _____
_____
_____

I had a medical appointment today and: _____
_____
_____

I felt loved and supported by: _____
_____
_____
_____

This is what I will remember most about today: _____
_____

# While I'm Still Here...Self-Reflections

Date:       /       /

My plans for today included:
_____
_____

The most challenging part of today was:
_____
_____
_____

**Today I feel:**
☐ At Peace
☐ Fearful
☐ Tired
☐ Lonely
☐ Reflective
☐ Forgiveness
☐ Anger
☐ Determined

I discovered that I enjoy: _____
_____
_____
_____

Today, I ate: _____
_____
_____

Today, I dressed up and felt: _____
_____
_____

I had a medical appointment today and: _____
_____
_____

I felt loved and supported by: _____
_____
_____
_____

This is what I will remember most about today: _____
_____

# While I'm Still Here...Self-Reflections

Date:      /      /

My plans for today included:
_____
_____

The most challenging part of today was:
_____
_____
_____

**Today I feel:**
- ☐ At Peace
- ☐ Fearful
- ☐ Tired
- ☐ Lonely
- ☐ Reflective
- ☐ Forgiveness
- ☐ Anger
- ☐ Determined

I discovered that I enjoy: _____
_____
_____
_____

Today, I ate: _____
_____
_____

Today, I dressed up and felt: _____
_____
_____

I had a medical appointment today and: _____
_____
_____

I felt loved and supported by: _____
_____
_____
_____

This is what I will remember most about today: _____
_____

# While I'm Still Here...Self-Reflections

Date:      /      /

My plans for today included:
_____
_____

The most challenging part of today was:
_____
_____
_____

**Today I feel:**
☐ At Peace
☐ Fearful
☐ Tired
☐ Lonely
☐ Reflective
☐ Forgiveness
☐ Anger
☐ Determined

I discovered that I enjoy: _____
_____
_____
_____

Today, I ate: _____
_____
_____

Today, I dressed up and felt: _____
_____
_____

I had a medical appointment today and: _____
_____
_____

I felt loved and supported by: _____
_____
_____
_____

This is what I will remember most about today: _____
_____

# While I'm Still Here...Self-Reflections

Date:     /     /

My plans for today included:
_____
_____

The most challenging part of today was:
_____
_____
_____

**Today I feel:**
☐ At Peace
☐ Fearful
☐ Tired
☐ Lonely
☐ Reflective
☐ Forgiveness
☐ Anger
☐ Determined

I discovered that I enjoy: _____
_____
_____
_____

Today, I ate: _____
_____
_____

Today, I dressed up and felt: _____
_____
_____

I had a medical appointment today and: _____
_____
_____

I felt loved and supported by: _____
_____
_____
_____

This is what I will remember most about today: _____
_____

# While I'm Still Here...Self-Reflections

Date:      /      /

My plans for today included:
_____
_____

The most challenging part of today was:
_____
_____
_____

**Today I feel:**
☐ At Peace
☐ Fearful
☐ Tired
☐ Lonely
☐ Reflective
☐ Forgiveness
☐ Anger
☐ Determined

I discovered that I enjoy: _____
_____
_____
_____

Today, I ate: _____
_____
_____

Today, I dressed up and felt: _____
_____
_____

I had a medical appointment today and: _____
_____
_____

I felt loved and supported by: _____
_____
_____
_____

This is what I will remember most about today: _____
_____

# While I'm Still Here…Self-Reflections

Date:      /      /

My plans for today included:
_____
_____

The most challenging part of today was:
_____
_____
_____

**Today I feel:**
- ☐ At Peace
- ☐ Fearful
- ☐ Tired
- ☐ Lonely
- ☐ Reflective
- ☐ Forgiveness
- ☐ Anger
- ☐ Determined

I discovered that I enjoy: _____
_____
_____
_____

Today, I ate: _____
_____
_____

Today, I dressed up and felt: _____
_____
_____

I had a medical appointment today and: _____
_____
_____

I felt loved and supported by: _____
_____
_____
_____

This is what I will remember most about today: _____
_____

# While I'm Still Here...Self-Reflections

Date:      /      /

My plans for today included:
_____
_____

The most challenging part of today was:
_____
_____
_____

**Today I feel:**
- ☐ At Peace
- ☐ Fearful
- ☐ Tired
- ☐ Lonely
- ☐ Reflective
- ☐ Forgiveness
- ☐ Anger
- ☐ Determined

I discovered that I enjoy: _____
_____
_____
_____

Today, I ate: _____
_____
_____

Today, I dressed up and felt: _____
_____
_____

I had a medical appointment today and: _____
_____
_____

I felt loved and supported by: _____
_____
_____
_____

This is what I will remember most about today: _____
_____

# While I'm Still Here...Self-Reflections

Date:      /      /

My plans for today included:
_____
_____

The most challenging part of today was:
_____
_____
_____

**Today I feel:**
☐ At Peace
☐ Fearful
☐ Tired
☐ Lonely
☐ Reflective
☐ Forgiveness
☐ Anger
☐ Determined

I discovered that I enjoy: _____
_____
_____
_____

Today, I ate: _____
_____
_____

Today, I dressed up and felt: _____
_____
_____

I had a medical appointment today and: _____
_____
_____

I felt loved and supported by: _____
_____
_____
_____

This is what I will remember most about today: _____
_____

# While I'm Still Here...Self-Reflections

Date:      /      /

My plans for today included:
_____
_____

The most challenging part of today was:
_____
_____
_____

**Today I feel:**
☐ At Peace
☐ Fearful
☐ Tired
☐ Lonely
☐ Reflective
☐ Forgiveness
☐ Anger
☐ Determined

I discovered that I enjoy: _____
_____
_____
_____

Today, I ate: _____
_____
_____

Today, I dressed up and felt: _____
_____
_____

I had a medical appointment today and: _____
_____
_____

I felt loved and supported by: _____
_____
_____
_____

This is what I will remember most about today: _____
_____

# Miss Me But Let Me Go
## by Christina Georgina Rossetti

When I come to the end of the road
And the sun has set for me
I want no rites in a gloom-filled room
Why cry for a soul set free?

Miss me a little-but not too long
And not with your head bowed low
Remember the love that we once shared
Miss me-but let me go

For this is a journey that we all must take
And each must go alone.
It's all part of the Master's plan
A step on the road to home

When you are lonely and sick of heart
Go to the friends we know
And bury your sorrows in doing good deeds
Miss me but let me go.

# Other Guided Journals & Diaries
## by
## Kinyatta E. Gray

**I Miss You...**

Daily Writing Prompts for Reflection, Remembrance, and Spirit Renewal

**Fashionista's Travel Diary**

A Guided Travel Diary for Travel Planning & Reflections

**I'm Doing Me**

The Ultimate Breakup Diary for Venting, Reflection & Spirit Renewal

**Kinyatta E. Gray** is a Best-Selling Author, Travel Influencer and the CEO of FlightsInStilettos, LLC. Kinyatta is also the Chief Beach Towel Designer for the FlightsInStilettos Glam Girl Beach Towels.

Websites:
https://www.flightsinstilettos.com/

https://www.kinyattagray.com/

https://www.honoringmissbee.com/

Disclaimer:

Kinyatta Gray is not a mental health provider and is providing this information based on her personal experiences. If you are experiencing an emotional crisis, seek the help of a professional mental health provider immediately.